The

KAMALA HARRIS

Biography

Kamala Harris's Journey of Justice, Equality, and Leadership

John Bison

Table of Contents

Introduction

In the pantheon of modern American history, few figures shine as brightly or as distinctively as Kamala Harris. Her ascent to the role of Vice President is not merely a personal triumph but a profound testament to the evolution of a nation grappling with its ideals and identity. Kamala Harris embodies the convergence of dreams, struggles, and hopes—a symbol of progress in a world often defined by its divisions. Her story is one of breaking barriers, challenging conventions, and redefining what is possible within the corridors of power.

Born into a world of complexities and possibilities, Kamala Harris emerged from a mosaic of influences that shaped her into the formidable leader she is today. Raised by a mother whose quest for knowledge and justice spanned continents and disciplines, Kamala's early life was imbued with a sense of purpose and possibility. Shyamala Gopalan Harris, her mother, was an acclaimed cancer researcher and civil rights activist, whose tireless work and unyielding spirit provided Kamala with an indelible example of what it means to fight for change. From her mother's stories of struggle and triumph, Kamala inherited not just the values of determination and integrity but also a profound understanding of the systemic issues that shape the world.

Kamala's upbringing in the diverse and vibrant city of Berkeley, California, further enriched her worldview. The environment around her was a crucible of activism and intellectualism, where the fight for civil rights, gender equality, and social justice was a daily reality. It was here that Kamala first encountered the complexities of societal inequalities and began to forge her path as a dedicated public servant. Her experiences as a young woman navigating these challenging landscapes were instrumental in shaping her approach to leadership—a blend of empathy, intellect, and unwavering commitment.

As Kamala embarked on her professional journey, her career was a tapestry woven with threads of legal acumen, advocacy, and an unrelenting pursuit of justice. Her tenure as District Attorney of San Francisco marked the beginning of her ascent onto the national stage. In this role, Kamala was a relentless advocate for the voiceless, working to reform a justice system that often failed to serve the most vulnerable. Her initiatives to tackle issues such as sexual violence and wrongful convictions were not mere policy measures but reflections of her deep-seated belief in fairness and equality.

Her subsequent role as Attorney General of California further solidified her reputation as a formidable force for change. Kamala's work during this period was a blend of innovative legal strategies and compassionate reform. She was instrumental in the fight against human trafficking, the promotion of reproductive rights, and the pursuit of economic justice. Her approach was both pragmatic and visionary, addressing immediate issues while also laying the groundwork for long-term systemic change.

Kamala's ascent to the U.S. Senate was a defining moment in her career. As a Senator, she leveraged her platform to tackle some of the most pressing issues of the time, from health care reform to criminal justice reform. Her legislative efforts were characterized by a blend of rigorous analysis and passionate advocacy, reflecting her commitment to creating a more just and equitable society. Kamala's ability to bridge the gap between policy and people, between analysis and action, marked her as a leader of remarkable capability.

The pinnacle of Kamala's political journey came with her historic election as Vice President of the United States. Her inauguration was not merely a ceremonial event but a profound milestone in American history. As the first woman, the first African American woman, and the first South Asian American to hold this office, Kamala's presence in the White House was a powerful symbol of the nation's evolving identity. Her vice presidency was characterized by an emphasis on collaboration, innovation, and a deep commitment to addressing both domestic and global challenges.

Kamala's impact as Vice President has been multifaceted. She has played a crucial role in navigating the complexities of the COVID-19 pandemic, advocating for economic relief, and addressing systemic inequities. Her work on climate change, international diplomacy, and women's rights has been marked by a blend of strategic insight and compassionate leadership. Kamala's approach to these issues reflects her belief in the interconnectedness of global challenges and the need for cooperative, inclusive solutions.

The story of Kamala Harris is not just one of personal achievement but of collective progress. Her career is a testament to the power of resilience, the importance of representation, and the impact of dedicated leadership. Kamala's journey from the streets of Berkeley to the heights of American political life is a powerful narrative of ambition, advocacy, and unwavering commitment to justice.

As we delve into the details of Kamala Harris's life and career, we uncover a portrait of a leader who has not only shaped the course of American politics but also set a precedent for future generations. Her story is a reminder that progress is possible, that barriers can be broken, and that the pursuit of justice is a continuous journey. Kamala Harris's legacy is one of hope, determination, and the relentless pursuit of a more equitable world.

This exploration of Kamala Harris's life is not merely an account of her achievements but an invitation to reflect on the broader themes of leadership, justice, and change. Her story challenges us to consider the ways in which we can all contribute to creating a better future, to confront the obstacles that stand in our way, and to embrace the possibilities that lie ahead. Kamala Harris's journey is a beacon of inspiration, a testament to the power of one individual's impact on the world, and a reminder of the enduring pursuit of a more just and inclusive society.

Chapter 1

Early Life and Family Background

Kamala Devi Harris, born on October 20, 1964, in Oakland, California, was destined to carve a significant niche in American history. Her roots, steeped in a rich blend of cultures, played a pivotal role in shaping her identity, worldview, and the indomitable spirit that would define her career. As the daughter of Shyamala Gopalan, a Tamil Indian breast cancer scientist, and Donald Harris, a Jamaican-born economist, Kamala's life was interwoven with narratives of resilience, intellect, and a relentless pursuit of justice.

Shyamala Gopalan's journey to America was emblematic of the dreams and aspirations held by many immigrants. Born in Chennai, India, Shyamala was the daughter of an Indian diplomat and a women's rights activist. Her early life was marked by a deep commitment to education and social justice, values she would later pass on to her daughters. At 19, Shyamala ventured to the United States to pursue her doctoral studies in endocrinology at the University of California, Berkeley. It was a bold move, reflective of her determination to break barriers when women, especially women of color, faced significant societal constraints.

On the other hand, Donald Harris hailed from Jamaica, bringing with him the vibrant cultural tapestry of the Caribbean. Born and raised in the rural town of Brown's Town in

Saint Ann Parish, Donald's early life was characterized by a pursuit of academic excellence. He eventually earned a scholarship to study economics at the University of California, Berkeley, where he would meet Shyamala. Their union was not merely a meeting of hearts but a convergence of intellectual rigor and a shared commitment to activism.

Kamala's childhood in Oakland was imbued with the spirit of the civil rights movement. Her parents were active participants in the struggle for racial equality, often bringing young Kamala to protests and community organizing meetings. These early experiences left an indelible mark on her, instilling a sense of justice and the importance of standing up for one's beliefs. Kamala and her younger sister, Maya, grew up in a household where the discourse at the dinner table ranged from discussions about social justice to the latest scientific discoveries, creating an environment that encouraged critical thinking and activism.

Despite her parents' eventual separation when Kamala was just seven years old, the values they instilled in her remained steadfast. Shyamala, now a single mother, took on the role of primary caregiver and continued to nurture her daughters' intellectual and cultural development. She ensured that Kamala and Maya remained connected to their Indian heritage, making frequent trips to India where the girls would spend time with their grandparents. These visits were more than just familial bonding; they were lessons in cultural pride and the importance of maintaining one's identity.

In addition to her Indian heritage, Kamala's upbringing was deeply influenced by her African American roots. Growing up in a predominantly African American neighborhood in Berkeley, she was immersed in the culture, traditions, and struggles of the black community. Her mother, recognizing the significance of this dual identity, often said, "You may be the first to do many things, but make sure you're not the last," a mantra that would guide Kamala throughout her life.

Kamala's early education began at Thousand Oaks Elementary School in Berkeley, a school known for its progressive values and diverse student body. This early exposure to a multicultural environment laid the foundation for her inclusive approach to politics and governance. Her teachers recalled her as a bright, inquisitive student with a keen sense of justice, often advocating for fairness on the playground.

The racial and cultural diversity of Kamala's early years was further broadened when Shyamala accepted a research position in Montreal, Canada. The family moved to Westmount, a suburb known for its academic excellence and affluence. Attending Westmount High School, Kamala faced the challenge of navigating a predominantly white, upper-middle-class environment. Yet, it was here that she honed her ability to bridge cultural divides, a skill that would prove invaluable in her political career.

Kamala's time in Montreal was marked by a balance of academic rigor and community involvement. She excelled in her studies, particularly in subjects that required critical thinking and analysis. Outside the classroom, she participated in debates and student government, showcasing her leadership potential. The cold winters of Montreal did little to dampen her spirit; instead, they forged a resilience that would characterize her approach to life's challenges.

Despite the geographical distance, Kamala remained deeply connected to her roots in Oakland and her extended family in India and Jamaica. Shyamala's commitment to cultural preservation meant that Indian festivals and traditions were celebrated with fervor in their home, while the vibrant rhythms of Jamaican music often filled the air. These rich cultural tapestries provided Kamala with a unique perspective on identity and belonging, allowing her to navigate multiple worlds with ease.

The dual influences of her Indian and Jamaican heritage, combined with the progressive values of Berkeley and the academic rigor of Montreal, created a multifaceted identity in Kamala. She was not just a product of her environments but an active participant in shaping them. Her childhood and adolescence were a blend of activism, intellectual curiosity, and cultural pride, all of which would become the bedrock of her future endeavors.

As Kamala transitioned from high school to college, her path seemed destined for greatness. She chose Howard University in Washington, D.C., a historically black university known for its legacy of producing

African American leaders. Howard was not just an academic choice but a deliberate decision to immerse herself in an environment that celebrated black excellence and nurtured future leaders. At Howard, Kamala thrived, majoring in Political Science and Economics, and becoming deeply involved in campus politics and activism.

Her time at Howard was transformative, solidifying her commitment to public service and social justice. Surrounded by peers who were equally passionate about making a difference, Kamala found a community that shared her values and aspirations. She joined Alpha Kappa Alpha Sorority, Incorporated, and the first historically African American Greek-lettered sorority, where she formed lifelong friendships and further developed her leadership skills.

Kamala's journey from Oakland to Howard, and eventually to UC Hastings College of the Law, was a testament to her unwavering determination and the strong foundation laid by her family. Each step of the way, she carried with her the lessons of resilience, justice, and cultural pride imparted by her parents. These early years were not merely a prelude but the crucible in which her character was forged, setting the stage for the remarkable career that lay ahead.

In her formative years, Kamala Harris was more than a student; she was a burgeoning activist, a bridge between cultures, and a young woman determined to make a difference. The values instilled in her by her parents, the experiences of her diverse upbringing, and the challenges she faced and overcame all contributed to shaping the leader she would become. Kamala's early life was a tapestry of rich cultural influences, intellectual rigor, and a steadfast commitment to justice, laying the groundwork for her historic journey into the annals of American history.

Chapter 2

Education and Formative Years

Kamala Harris's journey through education was a tapestry woven with ambition, resilience, and an unwavering commitment to justice. From her early days in Berkeley to her transformative experiences at Howard University, each phase of her educational journey contributed to the shaping of a formidable leader. The narrative of her education is not merely a chronicle of academic achievements but a profound exploration of her evolving identity, her growing awareness of societal injustices, and her unyielding resolve to make a difference.

Growing up in Berkeley, California, Kamala was immersed in a world where education was not just a privilege but a powerful tool for change. Her mother, Shyamala Gopalan, was a trailblazing scientist who instilled in Kamala the importance of knowledge and intellectual curiosity. Shyamala's work as a breast cancer researcher at the University of California, Berkeley, was pioneering, and her dedication to her field served as a constant source of inspiration for Kamala. The environment at home was one where books, discussions on scientific discoveries, and debates on social justice were commonplace, fostering a culture of learning and critical thinking.

Kamala's early education began at Thousand Oaks Elementary School, a progressive institution known for its diverse student body and inclusive values. The school's emphasis on equality and justice resonated deeply with Kamala, aligning with the principles she had been taught at home. Her teachers quickly recognized her sharp intellect and her innate sense of fairness, qualities that would become hallmarks of her personality. Kamala's time at Thousand Oaks was marked by her active participation in school activities, where she often took on leadership roles, advocating for her peers and standing up against any form of injustice.

As Kamala transitioned to middle school, her family moved to Montreal, Canada, where Shyamala had accepted a research position. The move was significant, not just geographically but culturally. Montreal's Westmount *neighborhood* was predominantly white and affluent, presenting Kamala with new challenges and opportunities. At Westmount High School, she encountered a different social landscape, one that required her to navigate cultural differences and assert her identity in an environment that was often unfamiliar. Yet, Kamala's ability to adapt and thrive was evident. She excelled academically, particularly in subjects that demanded analytical thinking and a deep understanding of societal structures.

Westmount High School was a place where Kamala's leadership skills blossomed. She became actively involved in student government, debates, and various extracurricular activities. Her peers often turned to her for guidance, recognizing her ability to mediate conflicts and articulate solutions with clarity and conviction. Kamala's experiences in Montreal were not just about academic growth; they were a training ground for her emerging role as a leader. The multicultural environment of Montreal, coupled with her Indian and African American heritage, enriched her understanding of identity and community, reinforcing her commitment to inclusivity and social justice.

The decision to attend Howard University in Washington, D.C., was a pivotal moment in Kamala's life. Howard, a historically black university, represented a return to her roots and a deliberate choice to immerse herself in an environment that celebrated black excellence. At Howard, Kamala found a community of like-minded individuals who shared her passion for activism and her drive to make a difference. The university's legacy of producing influential leaders in various fields provided Kamala with a sense of purpose and direction.

Majoring in Political Science and Economics, Kamala's academic journey at Howard was characterized by rigorous coursework and a deep engagement with the issues affecting marginalized communities. Her professors at Howard were not just educators but mentors who challenged her to think critically about the world around her. They encouraged her to question existing power structures and to envision a society where equity and justice prevailed. This intellectual stimulation was complemented by her active participation in campus politics, where she honed her skills in public speaking, negotiation, and advocacy.

Kamala's involvement with Alpha Kappa Alpha Sorority, Incorporated, was another significant aspect of her time at Howard. The sorority, with its long history of social activism and community service, provided Kamala with a platform to engage in meaningful projects that had a tangible impact on the community. Through her work with Alpha Kappa Alpha, Kamala organized voter registration drives, mentored young students, and led initiatives to address issues such as housing and education disparities. These experiences reinforced her belief in the power of collective action and the importance of uplifting marginalized voices.

One of the most transformative experiences during Kamala's time at Howard was her internship with California Senator Alan Cranston. Working in the Senator's office exposed her to the intricacies of legislative processes and the impact of policy decisions on everyday lives. Kamala's responsibilities included researching legislative issues, drafting policy proposals, and engaging with constituents. This hands-on experience provided her with a practical understanding of governance and the complexities of political decision-making. It also deepened her resolve to pursue a career in public service, where she could influence policies that addressed systemic injustices.

After graduating from Howard, Kamala's academic journey continued at the University of California, Hastings College of the Law.

Law school was a challenging yet enriching experience that further shaped her legal acumen and her commitment to justice. At Hastings, Kamala was known for her analytical prowess, her ability to dissect complex legal issues, and her unwavering commitment to fairness. She participated in moot court competitions, where her eloquence and strategic thinking earned her recognition and accolades.

Kamala's time at Hastings was not just about acquiring legal knowledge; it was about understanding the law's potential as a tool for social change. She was particularly drawn to courses on constitutional law, civil rights, and criminal justice, areas where she saw the greatest potential for impact. Her professors often spoke of her as a student who was not only brilliant but also deeply empathetic, always considering the human implications of legal doctrines and policies.

One of the defining moments of Kamala's law school years was her internship with the Alameda County District Attorney's Office. Working under the mentorship of experienced prosecutors, Kamala gained firsthand experience in the courtroom, handling cases ranging from minor offenses to serious felonies. This internship solidified her desire to pursue a career in criminal justice, where she could work towards reforming a system that she saw as deeply flawed and biased against marginalized communities.

Kamala's journey through education was a continuous process of growth, learning, and self-discovery. Each phase of her academic life added a new layer to her understanding of the world and her role within it. From the progressive values of Thousand Oaks Elementary to the multicultural environment of Westmount High, from the empowering community of Howard University to the rigorous training at UC Hastings, Kamala's educational experiences were instrumental in shaping her into a leader committed to justice, equality, and the betterment of society.

Her formative years were marked by a blend of academic excellence, community engagement, and a relentless pursuit of justice. Kamala's journey was not just about acquiring knowledge but about applying that knowledge to address the injustices she witnessed around her. Her education was a tool, a weapon in her fight for a more just and equitable society. Each institution she attended, each mentor she encountered, and each challenge she faced contributed to her evolution as a leader, preparing her for the monumental tasks that lay ahead.

Kamala Harris's educational journey is a testament to the power of knowledge, the importance of cultural identity, and the impact of community. It is the story of a young woman who, through determination, resilience, and an unwavering commitment to justice, transformed her educational experiences into a lifelong mission to create positive change. Her story is an inspiration, a reminder that education is not just about personal advancement but about using one's knowledge and skills to uplift others and make the world a better place.

Chapter 3

Rising through the Legal Ranks

Kamala Harris's ascent through the legal ranks is a narrative marked by determination, resilience, and an unwavering commitment to justice. Her journey from a young attorney in Alameda County to becoming the District Attorney of San Francisco, and eventually the Attorney General of California, is a testament to her legal acumen, her ability to navigate complex political landscapes, and her relentless pursuit of reform within a system often resistant to change.

After graduating from UC Hastings College of the Law, Kamala embarked on her legal career with a clear vision: to work within the criminal justice system and advocate for those who were often marginalized and voiceless. Her first significant role was as a deputy district attorney in Alameda County. The decision to start her career in the District Attorney's office was a deliberate one, reflecting her belief that real change could be effected from within the system. In Alameda County, Kamala was exposed to a wide range of cases, from minor offenses to serious felonies. This experience was invaluable, providing her with a deep understanding of the complexities and nuances of criminal law.

Kamala's time as a deputy district attorney was marked by her meticulous attention to detail, her ability to build strong cases, and her commitment to fairness. She quickly gained a reputation as a formidable prosecutor who was tough but fair. Her colleagues and supervisors recognized her potential early on, noting her ability to navigate the courtroom with confidence and poise. Kamala's approach to her cases was characterized by a deep empathy for the victims and a commitment to ensuring that justice was served. She believed in holding offenders accountable while also recognizing the importance of rehabilitation and restorative justice.

Kamala's success in Alameda County did not go unnoticed. In 2003, she decided to run for the position of District Attorney of San

Francisco. This decision was both bold and ambitious, as she was challenging the incumbent, Terence Hallinan, who was known for his progressive stances. Kamala's campaign was centered on the need for reform within the District Attorney's office. She promised to bring a new perspective, one that balanced the need for public safety with the imperative of ensuring justice for all. Her platform included initiatives aimed at reducing recidivism, addressing the root causes of crime, and implementing innovative programs to support victims.

The campaign was challenging, with Kamala facing significant opposition from those who were skeptical of her ability to lead. However, her tenacity, combined with her clear vision and compelling message, resonated with the voters. Kamala's grassroots campaign mobilized a diverse coalition of supporters, including community activists, legal professionals, and ordinary citizens who believed in her promise of change. Her victory in the 2003 election was a landmark moment, making her the first woman, the first African American, and the first South Asian American to be elected District Attorney of San Francisco.

As District Attorney, Kamala faced the daunting task of reforming an office that had been criticized for its inefficiencies and lack of accountability. She approached this challenge with the same meticulousness and determination that had defined her career thus far. One of her first major initiatives was the establishment of the "Back on Track" program, aimed at reducing recidivism among first-time drug offenders. The program focused on providing education, job training, and support services to help individuals reintegrate into society. Kamala's innovative approach garnered national attention and served as a model for similar programs across the country.

Kamala also tackled the issue of truancy, recognizing that chronic absenteeism was often a precursor to involvement in criminal activities. She launched a citywide initiative to address truancy, partnering with schools, parents, and community organizations. Her efforts included the implementation of a tracking system to identify at-risk students, as well as providing support services to families. The program's success in reducing truancy rates underscored Kamala's belief in addressing the root causes of crime rather than merely focusing on punitive measures.

During her tenure as District Attorney, Kamala also faced significant challenges, including high-profile cases that tested her resolve and legal acumen. One such case was the prosecution of Edwin Ramos, an illegal immigrant accused of the fatal shooting of a father and his two sons. The case attracted national attention and sparked intense debate over immigration policies and sanctuary city laws. Kamala's handling of the case was marked by her commitment to justice and her ability to navigate the complex legal and political landscape surrounding the issue. She balanced the need for accountability with a nuanced understanding of the broader implications of the case.

Kamala's success as District Attorney set the stage for her next major challenge: running for Attorney General of California in

2010. The race was highly competitive, with Kamala facing off against Steve Cooley, the District Attorney of Los Angeles County. The campaign was grueling, marked by intense scrutiny and political maneuvering. Kamala's platform focused on addressing the foreclosure crisis, reforming the criminal justice system, and protecting consumers. Her message resonated with voters, and she won a narrow victory, becoming the first woman, the first African American, and the first South Asian American to hold the office of Attorney General in California.

As Attorney General, Kamala's tenure was defined by her proactive approach to addressing some of the state's most pressing issues. One of her significant achievements was negotiating a $25 billion settlement with the nation's largest banks over mortgage abuses. The settlement provided relief to homeowners who had been victims of unfair practices during the foreclosure crisis, underscoring Kamala's commitment to protecting consumers and holding powerful entities accountable.

Kamala also focused on criminal justice reform, launching initiatives aimed at reducing recidivism, addressing the over-incarceration of nonviolent offenders, and improving police-community relations. She established the Division of Recidivism Reduction and Re-Entry to develop and implement strategies to help formerly incarcerated individuals reintegrate into society. Her efforts included advocating for the expansion of drug treatment programs, mental health services, and job training initiatives. Kamala's approach was holistic, recognizing that reducing recidivism required addressing the underlying factors that contributed to criminal behavior.

In addition to her work on criminal justice reform, Kamala also prioritized environmental protection and consumer rights. She established the Bureau of Children's Justice to tackle issues such as human trafficking, child exploitation, and foster care reform. Her office also took on major corporations, securing significant settlements in cases involving consumer fraud, privacy violations, and environmental violations. Kamala's tenure as Attorney General was characterized by her unwavering commitment to justice, her ability to build coalitions, and her innovative approach to problem-solving.

Kamala's rise through the legal ranks was not without its challenges and controversies. She faced criticism from both the left and the right, with some accusing her of being too tough on crime while others argued that her reforms did not go far enough. Despite the criticisms, Kamala remained steadfast in her belief that the criminal justice system could be both effective and fair. She navigated these challenges with grace and determination, always keeping her focus on the larger goal of creating a more just and equitable society.

Throughout her career, Kamala's commitment to justice was not just a professional mandate but a deeply personal mission. Her experiences as the daughter of immigrants, her exposure to the civil rights movement, and her work as a prosecutor all contributed to her understanding of the profound impact of the law on individuals and communities. Kamala's journey through the legal ranks was a reflection of her belief in the power of the law to effect change and her determination to use her position to advocate for those who were often marginalized and voiceless.

Kamala Harris's rise through the legal ranks is a story of perseverance, innovation, and an unyielding commitment to justice. Her journey from a young attorney in Alameda County to the highest legal office in California is a testament to her legal acumen, her ability to navigate complex political landscapes, and her relentless pursuit of reform. Kamala's legacy in the legal field is one of transformation, marked by her efforts to create a more just and equitable system for all. Her story is an inspiration, a reminder that with determination, resilience, and a commitment to justice, it is possible to effect meaningful change within even the most challenging and entrenched systems.

Chapter 4

Path to the U.S. Senate

Kamala Harris's journey to the United States Senate was a confluence of personal ambition, a deep sense of public duty, and an unwavering commitment to justice and equality. Her rise through the political landscape was marked by strategic brilliance, a tenacious spirit, and the ability to connect with a diverse electorate. As she transitioned from her role as Attorney General of California to a U.S. Senator, Kamala's path was paved with challenges, triumphs, and a relentless pursuit of meaningful change.

Kamala's tenure as Attorney General of California had established her as a formidable legal mind and a dedicated public servant. Her efforts to reform the criminal justice system, protect consumers, and champion environmental causes had garnered her national attention. It was during this time that Kamala began to consider the broader impact she could have on the national stage. The decision to run for the U.S. Senate was both a natural progression and a bold step, reflecting her desire to influence federal policies and advocate for the people of California on a larger platform.

The 2016 Senate race presented a unique opportunity. Senator Barbara Boxer, a longtime advocate for progressive causes, announced her retirement, leaving a coveted seat up for grabs. Kamala, with her impressive track record and growing popularity, emerged as a strong contender. The race was competitive, with multiple candidates vying for the position. Kamala's campaign strategy was rooted in her commitment to justice and equality, themes that resonated deeply with a diverse and progressive California electorate.

Kamala's campaign was characterized by its grassroots approach, emphasizing direct engagement with voters and building a broad coalition of support. She traveled extensively across the state, meeting with constituents from diverse backgrounds and listening to their concerns. Her ability to connect with people on a personal level, combined with her eloquence and command of the issues, made her a compelling candidate. Kamala's message was clear: she was running to be a voice for the voiceless, to champion progressive values, and to bring about real change in Washington.

One of the defining moments of Kamala's Senate campaign was her participation in a series of debates with her primary opponent, Congresswoman Loretta Sanchez. The debates showcased Kamala's sharp intellect, her deep understanding of the issues, and her ability to articulate a clear and compelling vision for the future. She tackled complex topics such as immigration reform, healthcare, and criminal justice with a nuanced perspective, highlighting her experience and her commitment to finding solutions that worked for all Californians.

Kamala's campaign also leveraged her unique background and identity, celebrating her Indian and Jamaican heritage and her role as a trailblazer for women of color. She often spoke about her mother, Shyamala Gopalan, and the values of resilience, justice, and public service that had been instilled in her from a young age. Kamala's personal story resonated with many voters, particularly those from immigrant communities who saw in her a reflection of their own struggles and aspirations.

The primary election results were a testament to Kamala's broad appeal and the effectiveness of her campaign strategy. She secured a decisive victory, advancing to the general election where she faced off against Loretta Sanchez once again. The general election campaign was intense, with both candidates vying for the support of California's diverse electorate. Kamala's message of hope, unity, and progressive change continued to resonate, and she maintained a steady lead in the polls.

On November 8, 2016, Kamala Harris made history by becoming the second African American woman and the first South Asian American to be elected to the United States Senate. Her victory was celebrated not only in California but across the nation, symbolizing a significant step forward for diversity and representation in American politics. Kamala's election to the Senate was a validation of her hard work, her dedication to public service, and her commitment to fighting for justice and equality.

As a U.S. Senator, Kamala hit the ground running, determined to make a difference on issues that mattered to her constituents. Her committee assignments reflected her areas of expertise and passion, including the Senate Judiciary Committee, the Homeland Security and Governmental Affairs Committee, and the Select Committee on Intelligence. These assignments allowed Kamala to play a critical role in shaping national policies on criminal justice reform, immigration, national security, and more.

One of Kamala's early priorities in the Senate was addressing the urgent issue of immigration reform. Drawing on her experience as the daughter of immigrants and her tenure as Attorney General, Kamala advocated for comprehensive immigration policies that balanced security with humanity. She championed the Deferred Action for Childhood Arrivals (DACA) program, fighting to protect young immigrants brought to the United States as children from deportation. Kamala's passionate defense of DACA recipients, often referred to as "Dreamers," highlighted her commitment to ensuring that America remained a land of opportunity for all.

Kamala's work on criminal justice reform also continued in the Senate, where she introduced and co-sponsored several pieces of legislation aimed at addressing systemic issues within the justice system. She worked tirelessly to end the use of private prisons, reduce mandatory minimum sentences for nonviolent offenses, and promote rehabilitation and reentry programs for formerly incarcerated individuals. Kamala's efforts were informed by her belief that true justice required a holistic approach, addressing the root causes of crime and providing individuals with the support and opportunities they needed to rebuild their lives.

In addition to her legislative work, Kamala quickly became known for her incisive questioning during Senate hearings. Her background as a prosecutor was evident in her ability to dissect complex issues, ask tough questions, and hold government officials accountable. Kamala's performance during the confirmation hearings of Supreme Court nominee Brett Kavanaugh was particularly notable. Her sharp, pointed questions and her unwavering commitment to seeking the truth earned her national recognition and solidified her reputation as a formidable advocate for justice.

Kamala's tenure in the Senate was also marked by her advocacy for healthcare reform. She supported efforts to protect and expand the Affordable Care Act, ensuring that millions of Americans had access to quality healthcare. Kamala introduced legislation to lower prescription drug costs, expand mental health services, and address the opioid crisis. Her approach to healthcare was holistic, recognizing the interconnectedness of physical health, mental health, and social determinants of health.

Throughout her time in the Senate, Kamala remained deeply connected to her constituents, regularly returning to California to meet with community leaders, activists, and everyday citizens. She held town halls, participated in community events, and maintained an open line of communication with her supporters. Kamala's commitment to being a responsive and accessible representative underscored her belief that elected officials must be accountable to the people they serve.

Kamala's journey to the Senate and her subsequent work were guided by a clear vision of a more just and equitable society. She understood the power of legislation to effect change, and she approached her role with a sense of urgency and purpose. Kamala's ability to build coalitions, her strategic acumen, and her unwavering commitment to her principles made her a powerful force in the Senate.

Her path to the U.S. Senate was a reflection of her broader journey: one marked by perseverance, resilience, and a deep-seated belief in the power of public service. Kamala's ascent through the political ranks was not just about personal ambition but about using her platform to advocate for those who had been historically marginalized and voiceless. Her story is an inspiration, a testament to the impact that dedicated and principled leadership can have on the world. Kamala Harris's rise to the Senate is a chapter in a larger narrative of hope, progress, and the ongoing fight for justice and equality in America.

Chapter 5

The Presidential
Campaign Trail

Kamala Harris's leap into the presidential race was a bold and ambitious move, one that epitomized her fearless approach to leadership and her deep commitment to fighting for justice and equality on a national stage. Her decision to run for the highest office in the land was driven by a confluence of personal conviction, political acumen, and a profound sense of duty to the American people. The journey was marked by exhilarating highs, daunting challenges, and a relentless pursuit of a vision for a more inclusive and equitable America.

Kamala's announcement to run for President came on January 21, 2019, Martin Luther King Jr. Day. This symbolic choice underscored her commitment to the principles of justice, equality, and civil rights that Dr. King championed. The announcement was made in front of a crowd of thousands in her hometown of Oakland, California, a city known for its rich history of activism and social justice. The enthusiastic response from the crowd reflected the excitement and hope that Kamala's candidacy inspired among a diverse coalition of supporters.

From the outset, Kamala's campaign was defined by its emphasis on justice, unity, and a commitment to addressing the systemic issues facing the nation. Her slogan, "For the People," encapsulated her lifelong dedication to public service and her determination to advocate for those who had been historically marginalized and voiceless. The campaign platform focused on a range of critical issues, including criminal justice reform, healthcare, economic inequality, and climate change.

Kamala's legal background and her tenure as California's Attorney General provided her with a unique perspective on the criminal justice system, and she used her campaign to advocate for comprehensive reforms. She proposed ambitious plans to end mass incarceration, eliminate private prisons, and promote rehabilitation and restorative justice. Her commitment to these issues was not just rhetorical; it was rooted in her extensive experience and deep understanding of the systemic changes needed to create a fairer and more equitable justice system.

Healthcare was another cornerstone of Kamala's campaign. She championed the expansion of the Affordable Care Act and proposed a plan for "Medicare for All," aiming to ensure that every American had access to quality healthcare. Kamala's approach to healthcare was holistic, recognizing the importance of mental health services, prescription drug affordability, and addressing the social determinants of health. Her comprehensive plan resonated with many voters who were concerned about the rising costs of healthcare and the need for a more equitable system.

Economic inequality and the need for a fairer economy were also central themes of Kamala's campaign. She proposed policies to increase the minimum wage, provide tax relief for working families, and invest in education and job training programs. Kamala's vision for the economy was one that prioritized the needs of ordinary Americans and sought to address the structural inequities that had left many behind. Her focus on creating economic opportunities for all, particularly marginalized communities, underscored her commitment to social and economic justice.

Kamala's campaign was also marked by her strong stance on climate change and environmental justice. She proposed bold plans to transition to renewable energy, reduce carbon emissions, and address the disproportionate impact of environmental degradation on low-income communities and communities of color. Her approach to climate policy was intersectional, recognizing the interconnectedness of environmental, economic, and social issues. Kamala's commitment to fighting climate change was both a moral imperative and a practical necessity, reflecting her understanding of the urgent need for action.

The presidential campaign trail was both exhilarating and challenging for Kamala. She crisscrossed the country, engaging with voters in town halls, rallies, and intimate gatherings. Her ability to connect with people from diverse backgrounds and listen to their concerns was one of her greatest strengths. Kamala's charisma, eloquence, and authenticity resonated with many voters, and her campaign events often drew large, enthusiastic crowds.

However, the campaign was not without its difficulties. Kamala faced intense scrutiny from the media and her political opponents, who questioned her record as a prosecutor and Attorney General. She had to navigate a crowded and competitive field of Democratic candidates, each with their own strengths and loyal supporters. The debates were a particularly challenging aspect of the campaign, as Kamala had to assert her vision and defend her record in a high-pressure environment. Her performance in the debates was generally strong, with memorable moments that showcased her sharp intellect and prosecutorial skills.

One of the defining moments of Kamala's campaign was her confrontation with Joe Biden during the first Democratic debate. Kamala challenged Biden on his past opposition to busing as a means of desegregating schools, a policy that had affected her personally as a child. The moment was powerful and emotional, highlighting Kamala's ability to speak truth to power and advocate for civil rights. However, the confrontation also sparked debate and controversy, with some questioning her motives and strategy.

Despite the challenges, Kamala's campaign continued to gain momentum, and she remained a prominent figure in the race. Her campaign's focus on justice, equality, and inclusive policies resonated with many voters, particularly those from marginalized communities. Kamala's ability to articulate a clear and compelling vision for the future set her apart from many of her competitors.

As the primary season progressed, it became clear that the path to the Democratic nomination was narrowing. Kamala's campaign faced significant financial and organizational challenges, and she made the difficult decision to suspend her campaign in December 2019. The decision was a pragmatic one, reflecting the realities of the political landscape and the need to prioritize the broader goal of defeating Donald Trump in the general election.

Kamala's decision to end her campaign was met with disappointment from many of her supporters, but it also underscored her commitment to the Democratic Party and the need for unity in the face of a common adversary. She pledged to continue fighting for the issues that mattered to her and to support the eventual Democratic nominee.

Kamala's endorsement of Joe Biden was a significant moment in the 2020 election cycle. Her decision to support Biden reflected a recognition of the need for experienced leadership and a commitment to defeating Trump. Kamala's endorsement brought renewed energy to Biden's campaign and signaled a unity within the Democratic Party.

The decision to select Kamala Harris as his running mate was a historic and strategic one for Joe Biden. Kamala's selection as the first woman of color on a major party's presidential ticket was a momentous occasion, reflecting the progress that had been made and the work that still needed to be done. The announcement was met with widespread enthusiasm and support, both from within the Democratic Party and from voters across the country.

As the vice-presidential nominee, Kamala brought a unique blend of experience, charisma, and policy expertise to the ticket. Her role in the campaign was crucial, as she engaged with voters, participated in debates, and helped to articulate the Biden-Harris vision for the future. Kamala's ability to connect with diverse communities and her unwavering commitment to justice and equality were invaluable assets to the campaign.

The 2020 general election was one of the most contentious and consequential in

American history. The Biden-Harris campaign faced unprecedented challenges, including the COVID-19 pandemic, economic turmoil, and widespread social unrest. Despite these challenges, Kamala's resilience and determination shone through. She campaigned tirelessly, advocating for policies that addressed the immediate needs of the American people while also laying the groundwork for long-term change.

Kamala's performance in the vice-presidential debate against Mike Pence was a highlight of the campaign. Her calm, composed demeanor and her ability to articulate clear and concise arguments contrasted sharply with Pence's evasiveness and often condescending tone. The debate reinforced Kamala's reputation as a formidable and capable leader, ready to step into the role of Vice President.

The election results on November 3, 2020, marked a historic victory for Joe Biden and Kamala Harris. The Biden-Harris ticket won with a record number of votes, reflecting the broad coalition of support they had built across the country. Kamala's election as Vice President was a landmark moment, breaking multiple barriers and setting a new standard for representation and leadership.

Kamala Harris's journey to the presidential campaign trail and her subsequent election as Vice President is a story of perseverance, resilience, and a deep-seated commitment to justice and equality. Her path was marked by challenges and triumphs, moments of profound significance, and an unwavering dedication to the principles that had guided her throughout her career. Kamala's ascent to the Vice Presidency is not just a personal achievement; it is a reflection of the progress that has been made and the work that still lies ahead. Her story is an inspiration, a testament to the power of determination, and a beacon of hope for future generations.

Chapter 6

The Historic Vice Presidency

Kamala Harris's historic election as Vice President of the United States marked a transformative moment in American history. Breaking multiple barriers, Kamala became the first woman, the first African American woman, and the first South Asian American to hold the office. Her journey to the Vice Presidency was a testament to her resilience, intelligence, and dedication to public service, and it signaled a new era of leadership and representation in the highest echelons of American government.

Kamala's inauguration on January 20, 2021, was a moment of profound significance. The sight of her taking the oath of office on the steps of the U.S. Capitol, administered by Supreme Court Justice Sonia Sotomayor, was a powerful symbol of progress and possibility. The significance of this moment was not lost on Kamala, who understood the weight of the expectations and hopes placed upon her shoulders. She was acutely aware that her ascension to the Vice Presidency represented not just her own achievement but the collective efforts and sacrifices of countless women and people of color who had paved the way.

From the moment she took office, Kamala was determined to make an impact. Her role as Vice President was multifaceted, encompassing both the traditional responsibilities of the office and a broader mandate to address some of the most pressing issues facing the nation. Her portfolio included tackling the COVID-19 pandemic, addressing systemic racism, combating climate change, and advancing economic equity. Kamala approached these challenges with the same tenacity and strategic acumen that had defined her career.

One of the first and most urgent tasks was addressing the COVID-19 pandemic. The Biden-Harris administration inherited a nation in crisis, with soaring infection rates, overwhelmed healthcare systems, and a struggling economy. Kamala played a crucial role in the administration's efforts to combat the pandemic, working closely with public health experts, coordinating with state and local governments, and advocating for a comprehensive federal response. Her background in public policy and her experience as a former Attorney General were invaluable as she navigated the complexities of the crisis.

Kamala's efforts were instrumental in the rollout of the COVID-19 vaccination campaign, which aimed to vaccinate millions of Americans in a matter of months. She traveled across the country, visiting vaccination sites, speaking with healthcare workers, and encouraging the public to get vaccinated. Her visibility and advocacy were critical in building public trust and ensuring that the vaccine reached underserved communities. Kamala's leadership during this challenging time underscored her commitment to protecting public health and her ability to mobilize resources and support in times of crisis.

Beyond the immediate crisis of the pandemic, Kamala was deeply committed to addressing systemic racism and promoting social justice. Her historic election had already sent a powerful message about the importance of representation, but Kamala knew that true progress required substantive policy changes. She worked closely with President Biden to advance a comprehensive agenda focused on equity and justice. This included efforts to reform the criminal justice system, protect voting rights, and address economic disparities.

Kamala's advocacy for criminal justice reform was particularly significant. Drawing on her experience as a prosecutor and Attorney General, she championed policies aimed at reducing mass incarceration, ending the use of private prisons, and promoting rehabilitation and reentry programs. She was a vocal supporter of the George Floyd Justice in Policing Act, which sought to address police misconduct and increase accountability. Kamala's work in this area was informed by her belief that true justice required systemic change and a commitment to addressing the root causes of inequality.

Voting rights were another critical focus for Kamala. In the face of widespread efforts to restrict voting access, she worked tirelessly to protect and expand the right to vote. Kamala led the administration's efforts to pass the John Lewis Voting Rights Advancement Act, which aimed to restore and strengthen the protections of the Voting Rights Act of 1965. She traveled to states with restrictive voting laws, meeting with community leaders and advocating for policies that would ensure every American had the opportunity to participate in the democratic process. Kamala's dedication to this issue was a reflection of her deep commitment to democracy and her belief in the fundamental right to vote.

Economic equity was also a central theme of Kamala's vice presidency. She worked closely with the administration to advance policies aimed at creating economic opportunities and reducing disparities. This included efforts to increase the minimum wage, expand access to affordable housing, and support small businesses. Kamala was a strong advocate for the American Rescue Plan, a comprehensive relief package designed to provide immediate economic support to individuals and families affected by the pandemic. Her focus on economic equity was driven by her belief that a just society required a fair and inclusive economy that worked for everyone.

Kamala's commitment to combating climate change was another defining aspect of her vice presidency. She played a key role in the administration's efforts to advance ambitious climate policies, including rejoining the Paris Agreement and setting bold targets for reducing carbon emissions. Kamala's approach to climate policy was intersectional, recognizing the interconnectedness of environmental issues and social justice. She advocated for policies that addressed the disproportionate impact of environmental degradation on low-income communities and communities of color, and she worked to promote a just transition to a green economy.

Throughout her vice presidency, Kamala remained deeply connected to the American people. She traveled extensively, meeting with constituents, community leaders, and activists to understand their concerns and advocate for their needs. Her ability to connect with people on a personal level, combined with her eloquence and empathy, made her a powerful and effective leader. Kamala's visibility and engagement were critical in building public support for the administration's policies and in advancing the broader agenda of justice and equality.

Kamala's role as Vice President also involved significant diplomatic responsibilities. She represented the United States on the global stage, meeting with foreign leaders, participating in international conferences, and advocating for American interests abroad. Kamala's diplomatic efforts were guided by her commitment to human rights, democracy, and global cooperation. She worked to strengthen alliances, address global challenges, and promote peace and stability. Her diplomatic skills and her ability to build relationships were invaluable assets to the administration.

One of the most significant moments of Kamala's vice presidency was her participation in the 2021 United Nations Climate Change Conference (COP26) in Glasgow, Scotland. Kamala's presence at the conference underscored the administration's commitment to addressing climate change and highlighted her leadership on the issue. She delivered a powerful speech, calling for urgent and collective action to combat the climate crisis. Her advocacy at COP26 was a reflection of her belief in the importance of global cooperation and her dedication to ensuring a sustainable future for all.

Kamala's vice presidency was also marked by her efforts to address the root causes of migration from Central America. She led the administration's efforts to develop a comprehensive strategy to address the factors driving migration, including violence, corruption, and economic instability. Kamala worked closely with leaders in the region, advocating for policies that promoted economic development, strengthened governance, and protected human rights. Her approach to immigration was compassionate and pragmatic, recognizing the complex and multifaceted nature of the issue.

Kamala's tenure as Vice President was characterized by her unwavering commitment to the principles of justice, equality, and public service that had guided her throughout her career. Her ability to navigate complex challenges, build coalitions, and advocate for meaningful change made her an effective and impactful leader. Kamala's historic election and her subsequent work in the Vice Presidency were a testament to her resilience, determination, and vision for a better future.

Kamala Harris's story is one of breaking barriers, challenging the status quo, and advocating for justice and equality. Her journey to the Vice Presidency and her work in office have inspired countless individuals and demonstrated the power of dedicated and principled leadership. Kamala's legacy is one of hope, progress, and the ongoing fight for a more just and equitable society. Her story is a reminder that change is possible and that with determination and courage, we can build a better future for all.

Chapter 7

Advocating for Women's Rights and Gender Equality

Kamala Harris's commitment to women's rights and gender equality has been a defining aspect of her career and her tenure as Vice President. Her passion for these issues is deeply rooted in her personal experiences, her professional background, and her unwavering belief in justice and equality for all. Kamala's advocacy for women's rights is not just a political stance; it is a fundamental part of who she is and what she stands for.

Kamala's early experiences shaped her understanding of the importance of gender equality. Raised by a single mother who was a prominent researcher and activist, Kamala grew up with a strong sense of the value of education, hard work, and social justice. Her mother, Shyamala Gopalan Harris, was a trailblazer in her own right, breaking barriers in academia and activism. She instilled in Kamala a deep respect for the power of knowledge and the importance of fighting for what is right. These lessons were foundational for Kamala and influenced her lifelong commitment to advocating for women and girls.

As Kamala progressed in her career, she encountered numerous challenges and obstacles that underscored the persistent gender disparities in society. Her experiences as a woman of color in the legal profession and in politics made her acutely aware of the unique struggles faced by women, particularly women of color. Kamala's resilience in the face of these challenges only strengthened her resolve to work towards a more equitable society.

Kamala's advocacy for women's rights took on new dimensions when she became the District Attorney of San Francisco. She implemented several initiatives aimed at supporting women and addressing gender-based violence. One of her notable achievements was the creation of a special unit dedicated to prosecuting sex crimes. This unit provided specialized training for prosecutors and worked closely with law enforcement and community organizations to ensure that survivors received the support and justice they deserved. Kamala's efforts to address sexual violence were driven by her belief in the importance of protecting the most vulnerable members of society and holding perpetrators accountable.

As Attorney General of California, Kamala continued to champion women's rights. She fought for equal pay, worked to combat human trafficking, and advocated for reproductive rights. Kamala's work on behalf of women was comprehensive and intersectional, recognizing the interconnectedness of various forms of discrimination and oppression. She understood that achieving gender equality required addressing the broader social, economic, and political factors that contributed to inequality.

One of Kamala's most significant contributions as Attorney General was her work to combat human trafficking. She launched initiatives aimed at prosecuting traffickers, supporting survivors, and raising public awareness about the issue. Kamala's approach to combating human trafficking was multifaceted, involving collaboration with law enforcement, non-profit organizations, and community leaders. Her efforts led to increased prosecutions and greater support for survivors, making a tangible impact on the lives of many women and girls.

Kamala's commitment to reproductive rights has been a consistent and central aspect of her advocacy for women. She has been a vocal supporter of a woman's right to choose and has worked tirelessly to protect access to reproductive healthcare. As Attorney General, Kamala defended California's reproductive rights laws against numerous legal challenges and worked to ensure that women across the state had access to safe and legal abortion services. Her dedication to reproductive rights is rooted in her belief that every woman should have the autonomy to make decisions about her own body and her own future.

As a U.S. Senator, Kamala continued to be a staunch advocate for women's rights. She co-sponsored several pieces of legislation aimed at promoting gender equality and protecting women's rights. One of her notable legislative efforts was the introduction of the Maternal CARE Act, which aimed to address the disproportionately high rates of maternal mortality among Black women. The bill sought to improve access to quality maternal healthcare, increase funding for training healthcare providers, and promote research on maternal health disparities. Kamala's work on this issue highlighted her commitment to addressing systemic inequities and improving health outcomes for women of color.

Kamala's advocacy for equal pay has also been a central focus of her work. She has been a vocal supporter of the Paycheck Fairness Act, which aims to close the gender pay gap and ensure that women receive equal pay for equal work. Kamala's efforts to promote pay equity are driven by her belief that economic justice is a fundamental aspect of gender equality. She understands that achieving equal pay requires addressing the broader structural barriers that contribute to wage disparities, including discrimination, lack of access to education and training, and inadequate workplace protections.

As Vice President, Kamala has continued to prioritize women's rights and gender equality. Her position has allowed her to advocate for these issues on a national and international stage, bringing greater visibility and urgency to the fight for gender equality. Kamala's work as Vice President has included efforts to advance policies that support women's economic empowerment, protect reproductive rights, and address gender-based violence.

One of Kamala's significant achievements as Vice President has been her work to advance policies that support women's economic empowerment. She has championed initiatives aimed at increasing access to affordable childcare, expanding paid family leave, and promoting workplace protections for women. Kamala understands that achieving economic equality requires addressing the systemic barriers that prevent women from fully participating in the workforce. Her efforts to promote economic empowerment are rooted in her belief that supporting women's economic security is essential for building a just and equitable society.

Kamala's commitment to reproductive rights has continued to be a central focus of her work as Vice President. She has been a vocal advocate for protecting access to reproductive healthcare and has worked to defend women's rights against numerous legal and legislative challenges. Kamala's efforts to protect reproductive rights are driven by her belief that every woman should have the autonomy to make decisions about her own body and her future. She understands that reproductive rights are fundamental human rights and that protecting these rights is essential for achieving gender equality.

Kamala's work to address gender-based violence has also been a significant aspect of her vice presidency. She has championed initiatives aimed at preventing domestic violence, supporting survivors, and promoting accountability for perpetrators. Kamala's efforts to address gender-based violence are driven by her belief in the importance of protecting the most vulnerable members of society and holding perpetrators accountable. Her work on this issue reflects her commitment to creating a society where all women can live free from violence and fear.

Kamala's advocacy for women's rights has also extended to the international stage. As Vice President, she has worked to promote gender equality and women's empowerment around the world. Kamala has participated in numerous international forums and has met with leaders from around the world to discuss strategies for advancing women's rights. Her efforts to promote gender equality on a global scale are driven by her belief that women's rights are human rights and that achieving gender equality is essential for creating a just and peaceful world.

Kamala's work to promote gender equality has been informed by her understanding of the interconnectedness of various forms of discrimination and oppression. She recognizes that achieving gender equality requires addressing the broader social, economic, and political factors that contribute to inequality. Kamala's approach to advocacy is intersectional, recognizing the unique challenges faced by women of color, LGBTQ+ individuals, and other marginalized groups. Her commitment to intersectionality is reflected in her efforts to promote policies that address the needs of all women, regardless of their background or identity.

Kamala's leadership on women's rights and gender equality has been a source of inspiration for many. Her ability to connect with people on a personal level, combined with her eloquence and empathy, has made her a powerful and effective advocate. Kamala's visibility and engagement have been critical in building public support for gender equality and in advancing the broader agenda of justice and equality.

Kamala Harris's story is one of resilience, determination, and a deep commitment to justice and equality. Her advocacy for women's rights and gender equality has been a defining aspect of her career and her tenure as Vice President.

Kamala's work to promote gender equality has made a tangible impact on the lives of many women and girls and has helped to advance the broader fight for justice and equality. Her story is a testament to the power of dedicated and principled leadership and a reminder that with determination and courage, we can build a better future for all.

Chapter 8

The Global Diplomat and Advocate

Kamala Harris's role as Vice President extended beyond the borders of the United States, embracing a broader vision of global diplomacy and international advocacy. Her tenure as Vice President has been marked by significant diplomatic engagements, strategic partnerships, and a commitment to addressing global challenges through cooperation and dialogue. Kamala's international work reflects her understanding that the issues facing the world today—climate change, economic inequality, and geopolitical tensions—require collaborative solutions and a steadfast dedication to human rights and democracy.

From the outset of her vice presidency, Kamala emphasized the importance of restoring America's relationships with its allies and partners. The previous administration's approach to foreign policy had strained many of these relationships, and Kamala, alongside President Biden, sought to rebuild trust and reaffirm the United States' commitment to its allies. She embarked on numerous diplomatic missions, meeting with leaders from around the world to discuss shared interests and challenges. Her approach to diplomacy was characterized by mutual respect, open communication, and a focus on building strong, sustainable partnerships.

Kamala's diplomatic efforts were guided by her belief in the power of multilateralism and international cooperation. She understood that addressing global challenges required working together with other nations, sharing knowledge and resources, and developing collective strategies. This belief was particularly evident in her work on climate change, one of the most pressing issues of our time. Kamala played a pivotal role in the United States' re-engagement with international climate efforts, including the Paris Agreement. Her advocacy for ambitious climate policies and her efforts to promote green technology and renewable energy were instrumental in positioning the

United States as a leader in the global fight against climate change.

One of Kamala's significant achievements in the realm of climate diplomacy was her involvement in the 2021 United Nations Climate Change Conference (COP26) in Glasgow. At COP26, Kamala delivered a compelling speech, calling for urgent action to address the climate crisis and highlighting the need for equity and justice in climate policies. She emphasized the disproportionate impact of climate change on vulnerable communities and the importance of supporting developing countries in their efforts to transition to sustainable energy sources. Kamala's presence at the conference and her advocacy for bold climate action underscored her commitment to creating a sustainable future for all.

Kamala's diplomatic efforts were not limited to climate change. She also focused on promoting economic development and addressing global inequality. She understood that economic stability and prosperity were essential for global peace and security, and she worked to advance policies that supported inclusive economic growth. Kamala championed initiatives aimed at reducing poverty, improving access to education and healthcare, and promoting gender equality. Her efforts to address economic inequality were driven by her belief that true progress required lifting up all members of society, regardless of their background or circumstances.

In her engagements with foreign leaders, Kamala emphasized the importance of human rights and democracy. She was a vocal advocate for democratic principles and the rule of law, and she worked to support countries facing authoritarianism and political repression. Kamala's commitment to human rights was evident in her efforts to promote press freedom, protect civil liberties, and support activists and dissidents around the world. Her approach to diplomacy was grounded in the belief that a just and peaceful world required the protection and promotion of human rights for all people.

Kamala's work on global health was another critical aspect of her international advocacy. The COVID-19 pandemic highlighted the interconnectedness of the world and the need for a coordinated global response to health crises. Kamala played a key role in the Biden-Harris administration's efforts to combat the pandemic, both domestically and internationally. She advocated for equitable access to vaccines, supporting initiatives to provide vaccines to low- and middle-income countries. Kamala's efforts to promote global health equity were driven by her belief that health is a fundamental human right and that no one should be left behind in the fight against the pandemic.

Kamala's diplomatic engagements were also marked by her efforts to address global conflicts and promote peace and stability. She worked closely with international partners to develop strategies for conflict resolution, support peacebuilding efforts, and address the root causes of instability. Kamala's approach to conflict resolution was informed by her understanding of the complex and multifaceted nature of global conflicts. She emphasized the importance of addressing underlying issues such as poverty, inequality, and political disenfranchisement, and she advocated for comprehensive and inclusive peace processes.

One of Kamala's notable achievements in conflict resolution was her work on addressing the crisis in Central America. She led the administration's efforts to develop a comprehensive strategy to address the root causes of migration from the region, including violence, corruption, and economic instability. Kamala worked closely with leaders in Central America, advocating for policies that promoted economic development, strengthened governance, and protected human rights. Her approach to the crisis was compassionate and pragmatic, recognizing the need for long-term solutions that addressed the underlying issues driving migration.

Kamala's diplomatic efforts also included a focus on strengthening international institutions and promoting global governance. She understood that addressing global challenges required effective and accountable international institutions, and she worked to support and reform organizations such as the United Nations, the World Health Organization, and the World Trade Organization. Kamala's efforts to promote global governance were driven by her belief in the importance of international cooperation and her commitment to building a just and equitable world order.

Throughout her vice presidency, Kamala remained deeply committed to engaging with the global community and advocating for policies that promoted peace, prosperity, and justice. Her ability to connect with people on a personal level, combined with her eloquence and empathy, made her a powerful and effective diplomat. Kamala's visibility and engagement were critical in building public support for the administration's foreign policy and in advancing the broader agenda of international cooperation and human rights.

Kamala's story is one of resilience, determination, and a deep commitment to justice and equality. Her work as Vice President has made a tangible impact on the lives of many people around the world and has helped to advance the broader fight for global peace and security. Kamala's legacy is one of hope, progress, and the ongoing fight for a more just and equitable world. Her story is a testament to the power of dedicated and principled leadership and a reminder that with determination and courage, we can build a better future for all.

Conclusion

As the pages of Kamala Harris's journey unfold, a portrait emerges of a leader whose life and career transcend the boundaries of mere biography. Her story is not only a chronicle of professional accomplishments and public service but a profound reflection of a personal mission to reshape the contours of justice and equality. Kamala Harris's legacy is intricately woven into the fabric of contemporary American history, and her influence extends far beyond the confines of her official roles, resonating deeply within the collective consciousness of a nation and beyond.

Kamala Harris's ascent to the Vice Presidency of the United States marked a transformative moment in history, embodying the culmination of years of dedication, perseverance, and visionary leadership. Her election was a testament to the evolving ethos of a nation striving to reconcile its ideals with its realities, and it symbolized the broader quest for representation, inclusion, and progress. Kamala's journey—from her formative years in Berkeley to the heights of the White House—reflects the relentless pursuit of an agenda defined by justice, equity, and reform.

In her tenure as Vice President, Kamala Harris has navigated a complex landscape of challenges with a blend of strategic acuity and empathetic engagement. Her work has spanned critical issues ranging from the fight against climate change and the pursuit of economic justice to the advancement of women's rights and the strengthening of international alliances. Kamala's approach to leadership is marked by an unwavering commitment to inclusivity, recognizing that the strength of a society lies in its ability to uplift all its members and address the multifaceted nature of its problems.

Her impact on domestic policy has been profound. Kamala's initiatives have sought to address systemic inequities and provide a voice to the marginalized. Her advocacy for affordable healthcare, educational equity, and criminal justice reform has been both innovative and impactful. She has approached these issues with a deep understanding of their interconnectedness and has championed policies designed to create lasting change. Kamala's leadership reflects a broader vision of a more just society, one where opportunities are not determined by one's background or circumstances but by one's potential and aspirations.

On the global stage, Kamala Harris has exemplified the principles of diplomacy and international cooperation. Her efforts to combat climate change, support global health initiatives, and promote human rights have underscored her belief in the necessity of a unified approach to the world's most pressing challenges. Her work has demonstrated that effective leadership requires not only addressing immediate concerns but also fostering long-term, collaborative solutions that transcend national boundaries. Kamala's global diplomacy is a testament to her understanding of the interconnectedness of our world and the need for collective action in the pursuit of shared goals.

Kamala Harris's story is also a narrative of personal resilience and determination. Her rise to prominence is a reflection of her ability to overcome obstacles, challenge conventions, and redefine expectations. Her journey has been marked by moments of triumph and adversity, each contributing to her growth as a leader and as a person. Kamala's experiences have shaped her understanding of the complexities of leadership and have reinforced her commitment to the values of justice and equity.

As we reflect on Kamala Harris's legacy, it is evident that her impact extends far beyond her official duties. Her leadership has inspired a new generation of leaders and has contributed to a broader movement for social change. Kamala's story is a source of inspiration and a reminder of the power of perseverance, vision, and dedication. It is a call to action for all who seek to make a difference in the world and a reminder that progress is achieved through both individual effort and collective action.

Kamala Harris's legacy is one of profound significance. Her contributions to American politics and global diplomacy are etched into the annals of history, and her influence will continue to resonate for years to come. Her story serves as a powerful reminder that the pursuit of justice, equality, and progress is a continuous journey, one that requires courage, conviction, and an unwavering commitment to the ideals of a better world.

In concluding this exploration of Kamala Harris's life and career, we are left with a deeper appreciation for the transformative power of leadership and the enduring impact of a life dedicated to service. Kamala's journey is a testament to the possibilities that arise when vision, determination, and empathy converge, and it stands as a beacon of hope and inspiration for all who strive to build a more just and equitable society.

Kamala Harris's legacy will be remembered not just for the milestones she has achieved but for the enduring values she has championed and the lives she has touched. Her story is a reminder that true leadership is defined not by the positions one holds but by the difference one makes in the lives of others. As we look to the future, Kamala's example will continue to inspire and guide those who seek to effect meaningful change and to contribute to a world that reflects the highest ideals of justice and humanity.

The

KAMALA HARRIS

Biography

**Trump Shifts Focus to Kamala Harris
after Biden's Withdrawal**

John Bison

Printed in Great Britain
by Amazon

9ad44483-6d60-4ae1-b726-2b3bbbd25846R01